CAN IT RAIN CATS AND DOGS?

QUESTIONS AND ANSWERS ABOUT WEATHER

W9-AZQ-281

BY MELVIN AND GILDA BERGER

ILLUSTRATED BY ROBERT SULLIVAN

SCHOLASTIC REFERENCE

Contents

KEY TO ABBREVIATIONS

cm = centimeter/centimetre
cm² = square centimeter/centimetre
g = gram
kg = kilogram
km = kilometer/kilometre
km² = square kilometer/kilometre
m = meter/metre
mm = millimeter/millimetre
t = tonne
°C= degrees Celcius

Text copyright © 1999 by Melvin Berger and Gilda Berger
Illustrations copyright © 1999 by Robert Sullivan
All rights reserved. Published by Scholastic Inc.
SCHOLASTIC and associated logos are trademarks and/or registered trademarks of Scholastic Inc.

No part of this publication may be reproduced, or stored in a retrieval system, or transmitted in any form or by any means, electronic, mechanical, photocopying, recording, or otherwise, without written permission of the publisher. For information regarding permission, write to Scholastic Inc., Attention: Permissions Department, 555 Broadway, New York, NY 10012.

Library of Congress Cataloging-in-Publication Data
Berger, Melvin.
   Can it rain cats and dogs?: Questions and answers about weather / by Melvin Berger and
   Gilda Berger: illustrated by Robert Sullivan.
          p.   cm.
   Summary: Provides answers to such questions about the weather as "What makes the
      weather?", "Does air have weight?", "How big are hailstones?", and "What is El Niño?"
   ISBN 0-590-13090-0 (pbk.: alk. paper)
   1. Weather—Miscellanea—Juvenile literature. [1. Weather—Miscellanea. 2. Questions and
   answers.] I. Berger, Gilda. II. Sullivan, Robert, 1970- ill. III. Title.
QC981.3.B465   1999   98-3042   CIP   AC

Book design by David Saylor and Nancy Sabato

10 9 8 7 6 5 4 3 2 1   9/9 0/0   01 02 03

Printed in the U.S.A.   08
First printing, March 1999

Expert Reader: Dr. Keith L. Seitter, Associate Executive Director,
American Meteorological Society, Boston, Massachusetts

To Marian and Martin, friends for all seasons
—M. AND G. BERGER

To Kerry and Danielle —
my true loves, my true inspiration
—R. SULLIVAN

Introduction

Why read a question-and-answer book?
Because you're a kid! And kids are curious.
It's natural—and important—to ask *questions* and
look for *answers*.

This book answers many questions that you may have:
- Why does the weather keep changing?
- What happens to puddles after it rains?
- Can you smell rain?
- Can lightning grow hair?
- Can groundhogs predict the weather?

Many of the answers will surprise and amaze you. We hope they'll tickle your imagination. Maybe they will lead you to ask *more questions* calling for *more answers*. That's what being curious is all about!

Melvin Berger   Gilda Berger

SUN, AIR, AND WIND

Can it rain cats and dogs?

No—but it can rain frogs and fishes! In the United States, frogs fell on Tennessee in October 1946 and on Arkansas in January 1973. Fish fell on Glamorgan, Wales, in 1859, on Frankston, Australia, in 1935, and on Louisiana in 1947—each during the month of October. Every time, rainstorms swept up the animals, which then came down with the rain.

People like to say, "It's raining cats and dogs" when it is raining very hard. The saying comes from an old belief that cats bring rain and dogs bring wind. But don't believe it. While it can rain frogs and fishes, it can't rain cats and dogs!

How does the tilt of Earth affect the weather?

It changes the amount of heat we get from the sun. When our part of Earth is slanted toward the sun, we get more heat. The temperature is generally high. It is summer.

When our part of Earth tilts away from the sun, we get less heat. The temperature is generally low. It is winter.

What makes the tropics hotter than the polar regions?

The direction of the sun's rays. The sun shines straight down on the tropics. The rays are very strong, making it very hot.

The rays from the sun strike the polar regions at a sharp angle. This spreads the rays out over a large area. It brings less warmth to the North and South Poles, leaving them very chilly, indeed.

How does air move?

Mostly in large blocks called air masses. Air masses move slowly from place to place. Wherever they go, they bring a change in the weather.

Cold, dry air masses form over cold land areas and generally move toward the equator. They usually bring clear, dry weather.

Cold, moist air masses form over cold ocean waters and also generally move toward the equator. They usually bring rain or snow.

Warm, dry air masses form over tropical lands and generally move away from the equator. They usually bring hot, dry weather.

Warm, moist air masses form over warm bodies of water and also move away from the equator. They usually bring clouds and rain showers.

What makes the weather?

The air. Planet Earth is surrounded by an ocean of air called the atmosphere. The layer closest to Earth is the troposphere. Here is where you find all of the weather—rain, snow, clouds, frost, winds, and so on.

The troposphere is only about 6 miles (10 km) deep. But it contains 80 percent of all the air. Above the troposphere the air gradually gets thinner and thinner to a height of a few hundred miles (km).

Why does the weather keep changing?

Because the sun heats the earth unevenly. Places around the equator—called the tropics—get lots of heat. The air in the tropics is always warm. Places near the North Pole and South Pole—called the polar regions—get very little heat. The air in the polar regions is always cold.

In general, air moves from where it is cold—the polar regions—to where it is warm—the tropics. The moving air creates the winds that make the weather change.

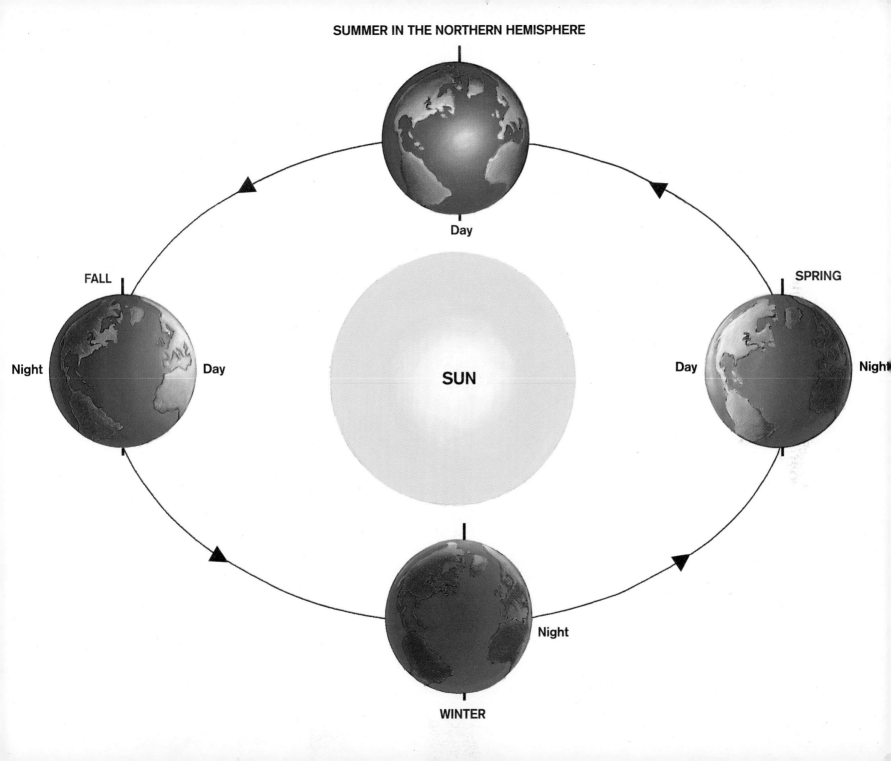

SUMMER IN THE NORTHERN HEMISPHERE

Day

FALL

Night   Day

SUN

SPRING

Day   Night

Night

WINTER

What happens when air masses bump into each other?

They form a front. Most changes in the weather happen along fronts.

You can see the moving fronts on a weather map. A line with red bumps shows a warm front, which often signals bad weather. A line with blue spikes shows a cold front. A cold front will cause bad weather as it passes, but good weather is often just behind it.

What happens when a warm air mass bumps into a cold air mass?

A warm front forms. The light warm air slowly slides on top of the heavier cold air. Clouds gather and rain or snow may fall. After a while, the warm front moves away. The sky clears, and the weather gets warmer.

Warm front

What happens when a cold air mass bumps into a warm air mass?

A cold front forms. The cold air slides in under the warm air. There are clouds, strong winds, thunderstorms, and perhaps heavy rain or snow. Soon the cold front passes. The rain or snow stops, and the sky clears. The weather usually gets colder. But watch out in winter! Icy winds can blow for days after the cold front has passed.

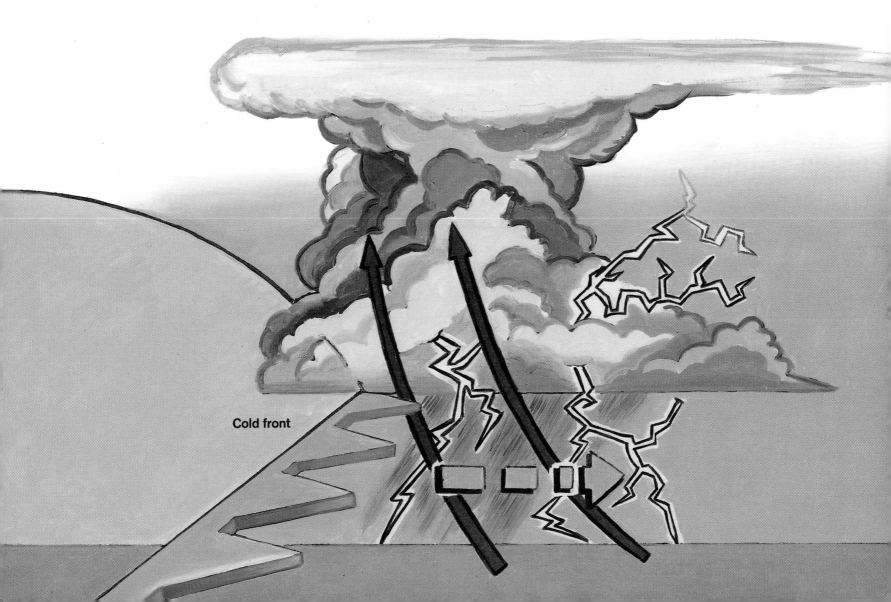

Cold front

How do you measure temperature?

With a thermometer. The thermometer has a thin column of liquid—usually colored alcohol, sometimes mercury. The level of the liquid changes as the temperature changes.

In warm air, the liquid in the thermometer expands and rises. In cool air, the liquid shrinks and drops. A temperature scale alongside the column of alcohol or mercury shows the temperature in degrees (°).

What is the hottest place on Earth?

The town of Al'Aziziyah, Libya. On September 13, 1922, the temperature in the shade reached a scorching 136 °Fahrenheit (58 °C)!

The record in the United States is held by Death Valley, California. The temperature there has reached 134 °Fahrenheit (57 °C). Every summer there is a race in Death Valley. But the ground is so hot that it sometimes melts the soles of the runners' sneakers.

What is the coldest place on Earth?

Vostok in Antarctica. On July 21, 1983, the temperature hit a bone-chilling minus 128.6 °Fahrenheit (-89.2 °C).

The lowest temperature in the United States—minus 80 °Fahrenheit (-62 °C)—was recorded in Prospect Creek, Alaska. Boil a pot of water in Prospect Creek and fling it into the air. You'll see the water turn instantly into ice!

Are mountaintops colder than valleys?

Yes. The higher you go in the troposphere, the colder you get. The temperature drops about 11 °Fahrenheit (6 °C) for every 3,300 feet (1,000 m). That's why people on a mountaintop can be shivering while people in the valley are trying to cool off!

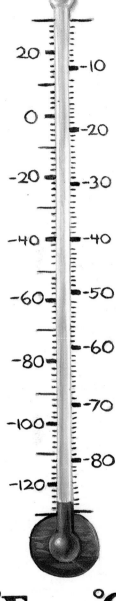

What is the difference between weather and climate?

Weather is the condition of the air and the atmosphere at one time and place. A summer hot spell and a sudden winter storm are examples of weather.

Climate is the usual weather in an area. Little rainfall on a desert and high temperatures around the equator describe climate.

Is Earth's climate changing?

Yes. It is always changing—but very slowly. Over the last 100 years the temperature has gone up about 1 °Fahrenheit (0.6 °C). Experts fear that the atmosphere may warm another few degrees in the twenty-first century. They call this global warming.

A few degrees may not seem like much of a change. But even a slight rise in temperature can increase rainfall, heat ocean waters, and melt polar ice. Over many years, global warming could force farmers throughout the world to grow different crops. And rising sea levels could flood the world's coasts.

What is the chief cause of global warming?

Widespread burning of such fuels as oil, coal, and wood. This adds vast amounts of carbon dioxide gas to the air. The carbon dioxide traps Earth's heat, which warms the surface and the atmosphere. Global warming is also called the greenhouse effect.

How can you slow down global warming?

Cut back on activities that require the burning of fuels. Walk or bike short distances instead of depending on car rides. Turn off lights when not in use to save electricity. And in the winter, dress warmly indoors so you can keep your house at a lower temperature and burn less fuel for heating.

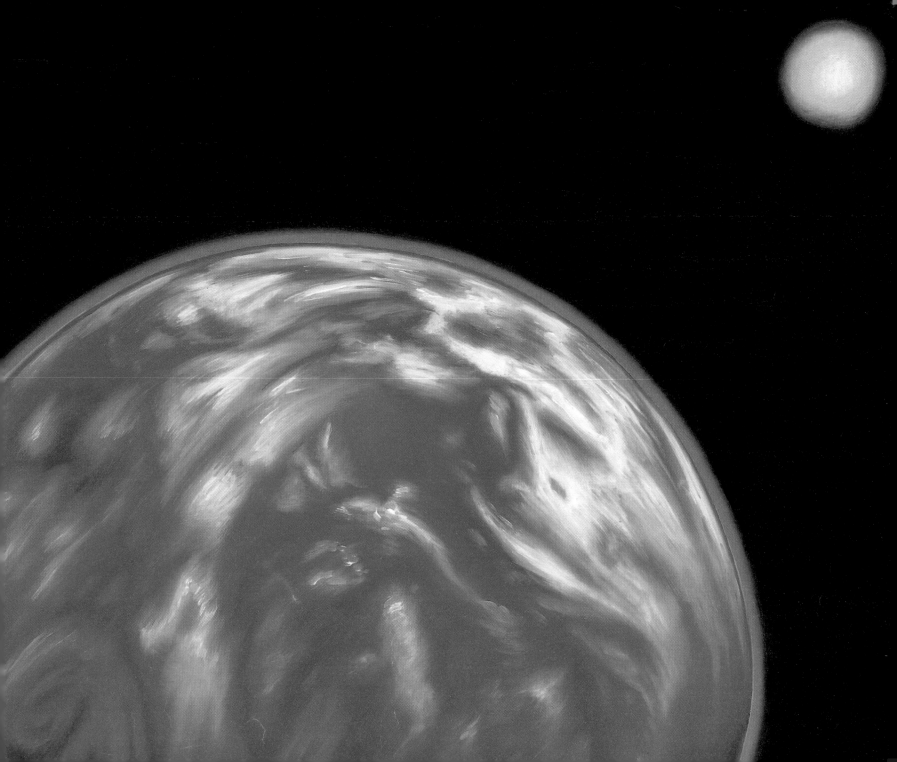

Does air have weight?

It sure does. Right now the weight of air on your shoulders is about 1 ton (1 t)!

At sea level, the air presses down with an average weight of 14.7 pounds (6.6 kg) on every square inch (6.5 cm²). This weight is called air pressure.

Why don't you feel air pressure?

Because air presses in all directions. The air inside your body presses out with the same force as the outside air presses in. Since the pressure inside is equal to the outside pressure—you don't feel a thing.

What happens to air pressure as you go higher?

It drops. The higher up you go, the less air there is above you. Less air pressing down means lower air pressure. For example, at the top of a 12,000-foot (3,658-m) mountain, the air weighs one-third less than at the base.

You can sometimes feel the pressure dropping as you go up in an elevator. Your ears pop as the air pressure inside your ears adjusts to the lower pressure.

Oddly enough, you don't feel a drop in air pressure inside an airplane that's taking off. That's because the pressure in the cabin is the same as the pressure on the ground. If not, your ears will pop!

Does air pressure affect the weather?

Yes. Low pressure and warm air masses usually bring cloudy weather and a chance of storms. High pressure and cold air masses usually signal clear, fair weather.

How do you measure air pressure?

With a barometer. The mercury barometer has a hollow glass tube set in a bowl of mercury. The air pressing down on the mercury pushes it up the tube about 30 inches (760 mm) or 1,000 millibars. In high pressure the mercury rises; in low pressure it falls.

The aneroid barometer is built around a metal box with most of the air removed. High pressure makes the box contract, low pressure allows it to expand. The change moves a needle over a dial. The dial shows you the shift in air pressure.

Which animals are "living barometers"?

Frogs. They can feel a drop in air pressure. As air pressure falls they croak more. A study in China shows that frogs are very accurate in sensing oncoming low pressure. So, if you hear frogs making more noise than usual, pack an umbrella!

What is wind?

Moving air. There is wind each time air flows from an area of high pressure to an area of low pressure. A big difference in pressure creates strong, gusty winds. A small difference brings winds that are light and breezy.

You can make a wind at home. Blow up a balloon. This puts the air in the balloon under high pressure. Now hold open the neck of the balloon. Feel the wind as the high-pressure air inside rushes into the low-pressure air outside.

Where are the windiest places in the world?

Commonwealth Bay, Antarctica, has winds that reach 200 miles (320 km) an hour. These winds blow for more than 100 days a year. Winds just one-third as fast would blow you off your feet!

The all-time record for wind over land was set on the top of Mount Washington, New Hampshire, on April 12, 1934. On that date the winds raced along at 237 miles (381.3 km) an hour. That's faster than the top speed of any car on the road today!

How do you measure the wind?

With an anemometer. The anemometer has three or four cups at the ends of rods that are attached to a central pole. The faster the wind blows, the faster the cups and pole spin. The speed of the spinning pole tells you the speed of the wind.

A weather vane shows wind direction. The simplest one is shaped like an arrow, pointed at one end and wide at the other. Set on a rod, the arrow turns freely with the wind. The wind blows equally on each side of the wide end. This turns the tip of the arrow to face into the wind. When the weather vane points north, you know a north wind is blowing. (A wind is always named after the direction from which it blows. A north wind blows from the north.)

Do winds always blow in the same direction?

No. Winds blow in all directions. But there are six bands of winds on Earth that generally blow the same way. They are called prevailing winds.

Prevailing easterlies blow from east to west around the North and South Poles.

Trade winds on both sides of the equator also blow from east to west.

Prevailing westerlies, which are between the prevailing easterlies and the trade winds, blow from west to east.

Which winds affect us the most?

Prevailing westerlies. They sweep over much of North America, Europe, Asia, and large parts of the other continents. These powerful west-to-east winds carry weather systems with them. People in New York often have the weather that people in Chicago had the day before.

Prevailing westerlies also speed up airplanes. It takes a half hour less to fly from New York to London (with the wind pushing) than to fly back (against the wind)!

Which winds helped Columbus?

The trade winds. They helped Columbus get to America! Columbus sailed west in the southern region of the Atlantic Ocean, where the trade winds blow. The winds filled the sails of the *Niña*, the *Pinta*, and the *Santa María* and helped speed these—and all other sailing ships—on voyages from Europe to the Americas.

What is the jet stream?

A fast-moving river of air high in the atmosphere that takes a wavy path from west to east. These powerful winds can reach speeds of more than 200 miles (320 km) an hour. Large weather systems tend to follow the direction of the jet stream. Locating the jet stream helps weather scientists, called meteorologists, predict changes in the weather.

WIND MAP

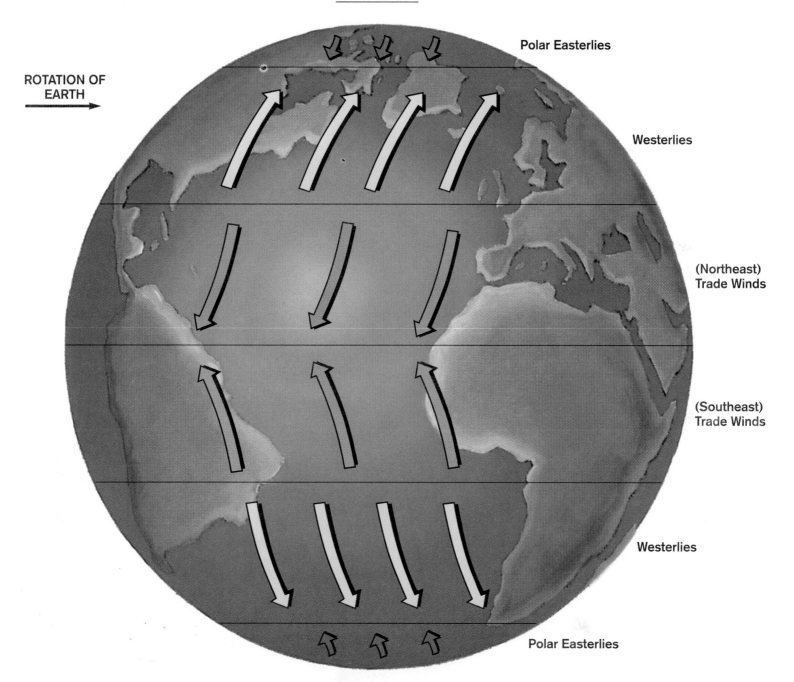

ROTATION OF EARTH →

Polar Easterlies

Westerlies

(Northeast) Trade Winds

(Southeast) Trade Winds

Westerlies

Polar Easterlies

Do other winds have names?

Yes. The chinook is a warm, dry wind that blows down the sides of the Rocky Mountains. It warms the plains east of the Rockies. The Santa Ana is similar to the chinook, but blows in the Sierra Nevada mountains of California.

A norther is a strong wind that blows from the north over the southern United States, the Gulf of Mexico, and the east coast of Central America. It can destroy boats and trees. During a norther the temperature drops very quickly.

The monsoon is a wind that blows across the Indian Ocean and some other warm areas of the globe. In the winter it blows from the land to the sea; it reverses direction in the summer season.

The sirocco is a hot, dry wind that usually blows north to Europe from the Sahara Desert. The wind is loaded with dust and sometimes brings rain.

The mistral is a strong, cold, northerly wind that blows down the Alps and across southern France. It may blow 100 days a year and cause frost damage to growing crops.

RAIN, SNOW, AND HAIL

What happens to puddles after it rains?

They dry up and disappear. Heat from the sun helps warm all the water on Earth's surface. It makes millions of gallons (liters) of water vanish from oceans, lakes, and rivers—and puddles. The liquid water becomes an invisible gas called water vapor. The change from liquid to gas is called evaporation.

Where does the water vapor go?

It mixes in with the air. You can't see it, you can't feel it, you can't smell it—but it's there.

The air with the water vapor rises as it is warmed by the sun. As the moist, warm air rises higher, it gets colder. In time, it gets so cold that the water vapor changes into tiny droplets, or raindrops, of water. We call this condensation. If it's very cold, the water vapor forms little ice crystals instead of raindrops.

What is at the center of every raindrop?

A tiny bit of dust. The water vapor condenses around a speck of dust, which is at the center of the raindrop.

Are raindrops shaped like tears?

No. Raindrops are round. But as the drops fall, they may flatten out a bit—looking more like tiny hamburger buns.

In a heavy rain, the drops are about 0.2 inch (0.5 cm) across. These big raindrops fall at a speed of about 20 feet (6 m) a second. Smaller drops, called drizzle, may take an hour to fall to Earth!

Clouds form.

Raindrops form
and fall to Earth.

The sun's heat
causes evaporation.

Water vapor rises.

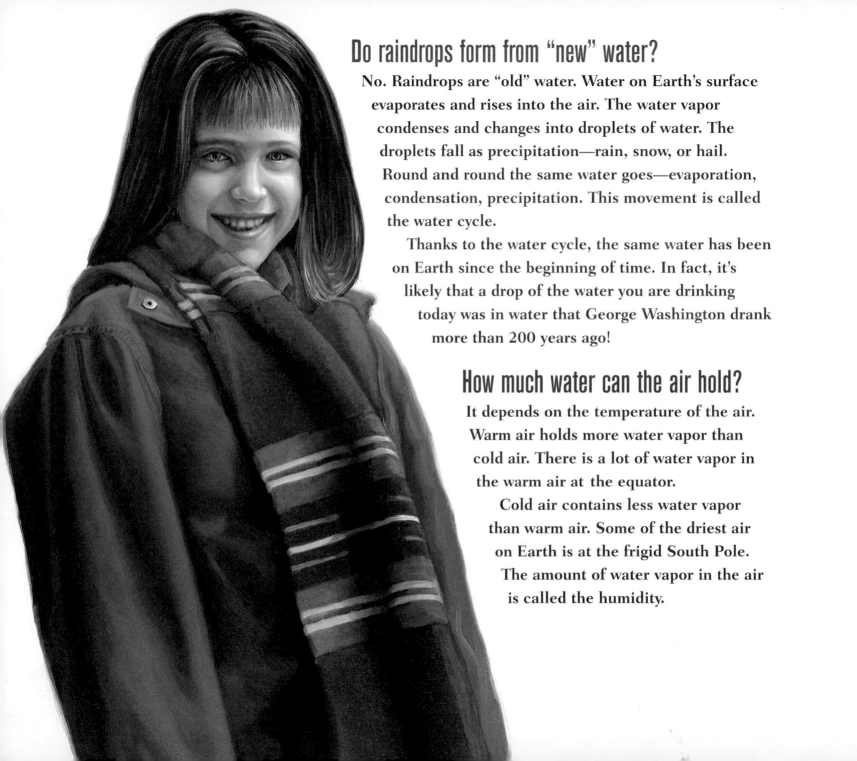

Do raindrops form from "new" water?

No. Raindrops are "old" water. Water on Earth's surface evaporates and rises into the air. The water vapor condenses and changes into droplets of water. The droplets fall as precipitation—rain, snow, or hail. Round and round the same water goes—evaporation, condensation, precipitation. This movement is called the water cycle.

Thanks to the water cycle, the same water has been on Earth since the beginning of time. In fact, it's likely that a drop of the water you are drinking today was in water that George Washington drank more than 200 years ago!

How much water can the air hold?

It depends on the temperature of the air. Warm air holds more water vapor than cold air. There is a lot of water vapor in the warm air at the equator.

Cold air contains less water vapor than warm air. Some of the driest air on Earth is at the frigid South Pole. The amount of water vapor in the air is called the humidity.

How do you measure humidity?

With a hygrometer. This instrument uses human hair.
It works because hair gets longer in high humidity
and shorter in lower humidity.

The hygrometer holds one end of several hairs in a
clamp. The other ends are attached to a pointer over a
dial. As the humidity goes up or down, the hairs change
length. This moves the pointer. You read the dial to
discover the humidity.

What do air conditioners do?

Chill the air. Cool air can't hold as much moisture as
warm air. The water vapor condenses into drops of
liquid water. This lowers the humidity. The air
becomes not only cooler but drier. We feel less soggy.

When do you use humidifiers?

In winter. Humidifiers add water vapor to the air
in your home. Air that is cold has very low
humidity. And heating your home dries out the
air even more.

Humid air is better to breathe because it
moistens the linings of your nose and throat.
The moist linings help to fight off germs that
cause colds and sore throats.

What makes clouds?

Tiny droplets of water or crystals of ice. Water vapor rises in the air. It cools and condenses into droplets of water. If the air is very cold, the water vapor changes directly into little crystals of ice. A cloud forms when enough water vapor has condensed into billions of droplets or ice crystals.

Why do clouds have different shapes and colors?

Because clouds form in various ways. White and fluffy cumulus clouds form when warm, moist air rises quickly from the ground and is cooled fast. Cumulus clouds look like heaps of cotton balls.

Cirrus clouds form so high in the sky that they contain only ice crystals. They are light and wispy, and look like feathers or curls of hair.

When air rises very slowly over a large area, low layers of clouds form. They look like heavy, gray blankets stretched over vast areas of the sky.

How long do clouds last?

Less time than you might think. An average cumulus cloud breaks up in about 10 minutes! Watch a cloud sometime on a summer afternoon and you'll see.

Is fog the same as clouds?

The same—and different. Both fog and clouds consist of tiny droplets of water. But clouds form high in the sky. Fog forms at ground level.

You get fog on calm, cool nights when the ground is cold. The water vapor in the air condenses into droplets of water. Fog forms as the air near the ground fills with these droplets. The drops are so tiny, it takes about 7 trillion to make 1 tablespoon of water!

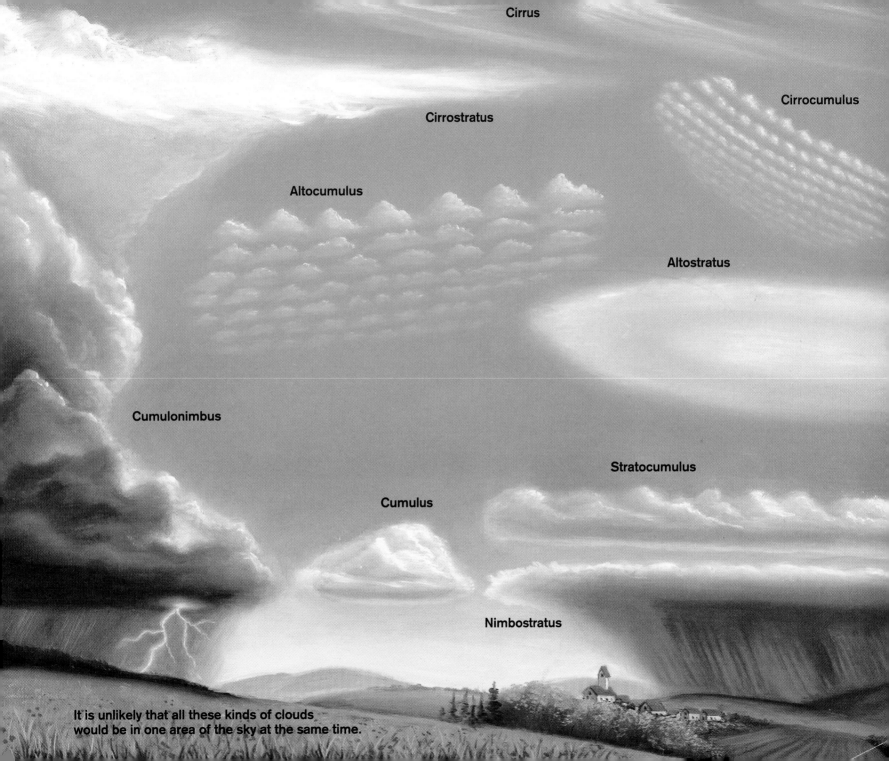

Cirrus

Cirrostratus

Cirrocumulus

Altocumulus

Altostratus

Cumulonimbus

Stratocumulus

Cumulus

Nimbostratus

It is unlikely that all these kinds of clouds would be in one area of the sky at the same time.

Can you smell rain?

Sometimes. Plants always give off a certain oil. When rain is coming, there is a drop in air pressure, and the air picks up a trace of the oil's odor. One sniff and you may be able to tell that rain is on the way.

Your sense of smell also is sharpest when the air is moist. Breathe deeply on the next damp day. You may even pick up the weak smell of soggy soil.

Does rain fall evenly all over Earth?

No. Some places go long periods with little or no rain. This is called a drought. The worst drought in history was in Calama, Chile. No rain fell from 1572 until 1972! Finally people's prayers were answered. It rained—but the terrible downpour damaged every single building in town!

Other places have too much rain. Mount Wai-'ale-'ale in Kauai, Hawaii, has the greatest number of rainy days each year. It rains 350 days a year!

How do you measure rainfall?

With a rain gauge. This tool looks like an open tin can. Inside, a funnel empties into a narrow, hollow tube. Rain falls into the funnel and flows into the tube. A scale shows you the rainfall in inches (cm).

Meghalaya, India, is the wettest place in the world. Meteorologists here must have extra-big rain gauges. Every year Meghalaya gets about 467 inches (1,186 cm) of rainfall! Compare this with the world average of only 34 inches (86 cm) a year.

When do you see a rainbow?

When the sun comes out after a morning or late-afternoon shower. Sunlight looks white. But it is really made up of many different colors. The sun's rays strike the drops of rain in the sky. This breaks the white light into the colors of the rainbow—red, orange, yellow, green, blue, indigo, and violet.

What is snow?

Ice crystals that form when it is too cold for raindrops to form. At these low temperatures, the water vapor in the clouds condenses into ice crystals. The ice crystals fall as soft, white flakes that we call snow. Like every raindrop, each snow crystal or snowflake forms around a tiny bit of dust.

Are two snowflakes ever the same?

No. Every snowflake has six sides. But you'll never find two that are exactly alike!

The shape of the snowflake depends on the temperature of the air. In very, very cold air, you'll find more needle and rod shapes. If it's less cold, the snowflakes take on more complicated forms.

Is snow always white?

No. Red snow fell in Switzerland in October 1755. The color came from red sand that blew over from the Sahara Desert. In January 1925, a layer of gray snow covered parts of Japan. It was probably colored gray by dust from an erupting volcano. In December 1926, black snow fell in France. Alas, no one knows why.

How do you measure snow?

With a snowstick. A snowstick is simply a ruler that measures the depth of the snow.

You can also melt the snow and measure how much water you have. Six inches (15 cm) of wet snow or 30 inches (76 cm) of dry, fluffy snow melts down to 1 inch (2.5 cm) of water.

Do snowflakes melt as they fall?

Quite often. Sometimes the snowflakes fall through warmer air. They melt and fall to Earth as rain. Other times the snowflakes melt, and then pass through colder air, where they freeze again. Then they form sleet. Sleet is made up of balls of clear ice, each one less than .2 inches (5 mm) across.

What is a blizzard?

A snowstorm with very strong, cold winds. In a blizzard, the winds gust 35 miles (56 km) an hour or more, the temperature falls below 20 °Fahrenheit (-6.6 °C), and blowing snow cuts visibility to less than .25 miles (0.4 km).

When does it hail?

Usually during the spring and summer. Hail starts to form when powerful winds blow raindrops 2 or 3 miles (3.2 or 4.8 km) up into the air. It is so cold there that the drops form into balls of ice, called hailstones.

As the hailstones fall, they get covered with water. But then, winds blow them up again. More ice forms on the hailstones. This happens over and over again. Finally, the hailstones are covered with many coats of ice. They fall to Earth in a hailstorm.

How big are hailstones?

Most are the size and shape of small peas. But once in a while hailstones get quite large. In May 1926, hailstones the size of baseballs fell in Dallas, Texas. In just 15 minutes the hail caused $2 million in damage!

The biggest hailstone on record was as big as a medium-sized pumpkin. This hailstone—17.5 inches (44.5 cm) around and weighing 1.6 pounds (753 g)—fell in Coffeyville, Kansas, on September 3, 1970. Luckily, it didn't land on anyone's head!

Sad to say, the hailstones that fell on Bangladesh on April 14, 1986, were another story. Some weighed up to 2.2 pounds (1 kg)! The giant chunks of ice killed nearly 100 people.

What makes dew come—and go?

Condensation and evaporation. On cool nights the ground is cold enough to condense part of the water vapor in the air. It becomes shiny drops of water, or dew. The dew forms on objects near the ground—grass and plants, signs and fences, buildings and cars.

In the morning, the sun rises and warms the ground and the air just above it. The dew evaporates. It changes back into water vapor—and is gone!

Who is Jack Frost?

An imaginary character who is said to cover things with a thin layer of ice, or frost. If you wake one morning and see an ice-covered world, you know you've had a visit from Jack Frost!

Frost forms just like dew, but only on nights when the temperature is below 32 °Fahrenheit (0 °C). The water vapor freezes on the ground and on windows, cars, and trees. Take care! Jack Frost can make you slip and slide when you go out.

WILD WEATHER

What is lightning?

A giant spark that flashes across the sky. Each bolt zigzags through the air at many thousands of miles (km) a second! Its electrical charge of about 100 million volts would be enough to light a small town for a whole year!

The charge comes from tiny drops of water or ice that bump and rub within huge, towering cumulonimbus clouds. When the charge gets big enough, it creates the lightning. Bolts jump between the cloud and the ground or between two clouds.

How often does lightning occur?

At this moment, meteorologists are tracking nearly 2,000 lightning storms around the world! These storms are hurling about 100 bolts of lightning toward Earth every second.

The city of Bogor, Java, holds the record for most lightning. It has lightning almost 9 out of every 10 days!

What causes thunder?

Lightning. The roar of thunder comes from the heat of lightning. The blazing bolt instantly heats the surrounding air to more than 60,000 °Fahrenheit (33,315 °C). The sudden burst of heat makes the air explode out. That makes the crashing sounds of thunder.

Thunder can hurt your ears. But you're not even hearing the entire sound. Most of it is too low for your ears to pick up. Still, you know it's there. You can feel the house vibrate and the dishes and windows rattle.

Can you have thunder without lightning?

Never. Thunder and lightning always come together. But you'd never know it. You always see the lightning before you hear the thunder. That's because light travels super fast, at 186,000 miles (300,000 km) a second! Sound is much slower, at only about 0.2 miles (0.3 km) a second. So first you see the lightning, then you hear the thunder.

How can you tell the distance to lightning?

Count the seconds between the flash of lightning and the sound of thunder. If you hear the thunder five seconds after you see the lightning, the lightning is 1 mile (1.6 km) away. Ten seconds means the lightning is 2 miles (3.2 km) away. And so on.

Is lightning dangerous?

Terribly. Lightning is attracted to tall trees or buildings and water. So stay away from trees and stop swimming during a thunderstorm. If you can, stay indoors and don't use the telephone. If you're in a car, wait there. Lightning passes around the outside of a car and through the tires into the ground. You'll be safe inside.

Does lightning ever strike twice in the same place?

Definitely. The Empire State Building may be hit as many as 12 times in just one 20-minute thunderstorm! It is struck up to 500 times a year. But no harm is done. The building has lightning rods that carry the electricity safely to the ground.

The tallest building in Venice, Italy, is the bell tower of Saint Mark's Cathedral. Lightning bolts seriously damaged the bell tower at least four times—in 1388, 1417, 1489, and 1745.

Who is called the "human lightning rod"?

Ray Sullivan. He was a forest ranger in Virginia who was struck by lightning an amazing seven times between 1942 and 1977!

The first time, Sullivan lost a big toenail. Twice the lightning set his hair on fire. Other times the heat burned his forehead, shoulders, legs, and chest. The last bolt landed Sullivan in the hospital. However, most people who are struck by lightning are killed the first time.

Can lightning grow hair?

Maybe. Edwin Robinson, age 53, had been bald for many years. On June 4, 1980, he was struck by lightning and was knocked out for 20 minutes. Two months later his hair started growing again. Another mystery of science!

What is the most powerful and destructive of all storms?

A hurricane. An average hurricane lasts about 10 days and travels over hundreds of miles (km). Most of the time, hurricanes rage over oceans. But they often pass over islands or coastal areas. The hurricane's forceful winds and drenching rains may take many lives and cause widespread damage.

Where do hurricanes start?

In an area of low air pressure over a warm, tropical sea. If conditions are right, strong winds begin to blow. They pick up more and more force. Presently, the powerful gusts and heavy rains produce a tropical storm.

Over the next day or two, the storm conditions may grow worse. The swirling winds can reach speeds of more than 74 miles (119 km) an hour. Torrents of rain gush down. The tropical storm has become a hurricane!

Hurricanes swirl around a central eye. As the eye passes overhead, there is a lull in the stormy conditions. But then the fury of the storm returns. The fiercest winds and heaviest rains occur within the wall of clouds that surround the eye.

Hurricanes originate in the Caribbean Sea, the Gulf of Mexico, or the Atlantic Ocean. If they form in the Pacific Ocean off the coast of Asia, people call them typhoons. The same hurricanes in the Indian Ocean are called cyclones.

How do hurricanes get their names?

From an alphabetical list that meteorologists prepare each year. Originally, hurricanes were named after famous people that a meteorologist disliked. Later, meteorologists drew up lists of women's names. When asked why they used women's names, one meteorologist joked, "Because they're 'her-icanes,' not 'his-icanes'!" Today hurricanes are given the names of both men and women.

The one that slammed into the city of Galveston, Texas, in September 1900. The hurricane sent huge waves crashing onto land and dropped tons of rain. The result was a flood that covered the city with 16 feet (5 m) of water—and a death toll of around 6,000.

The most costly hurricane was Hurricane Andrew. It roared across Florida and Louisiana in August 1992. Among its effects were 76 dead, 258,000 homeless, and $47 billion in damage!

What storm is smaller than a hurricane—but much more violent?

A tornado, or twister. The winds around the center of a tornado are the fastest winds on Earth. They can reach speeds of more than 200 miles (320 km) an hour! Winds at that speed can do everything from knock over trees and buildings to pick up big, heavy trains and trucks.

Do tornadoes make houses explode?

No. But it sure looks that way. Tornado winds push against one side of a building. They force air into the building. Then, the building starts to collapse. At the same time, the opposite wall seems to explode out. But it's the high air pressure inside the house, not the tornado itself, that knocks out the walls.

If you're in a building when a tornado is coming, hide in the basement. That will keep you safe—even if the rest of the house blows away.

Why are tornado winds dark in color?

Because they are filled with dirt. Tornado winds suck up everything they touch. They're soon filled with soil, dust, and debris. All this stuff makes the tornado winds turn dark and murky.

When do tornadoes strike?

All year long. But most come during the months of April, May, and June. The fewest are in December and January.

About four out of every five tornadoes form in the afternoon or evening. The worst time is between four o'clock and six o'clock in the afternoon.

Tornadoes strike all over the world. But the United States holds the record—an average of 700 a year. Texas leads the other states with about 115 tornadoes a year. But in 1967, Texas outdid itself with 232 twisters!

Which tornado broke all the records?

The tornado of March 18, 1925, which swept over Missouri, Illinois, and Indiana. It set the record for:

- Longest path—220 miles (352 km).
- Greatest width—1 mile (1.6 km).
- Longest lasting—3½ hours.
- Biggest area of destruction—164 square miles (425 km²).
- Most injured—nearly 2,000.
- Most killed—nearly 700.

Do mobile homes attract twisters?

No. But mobile homes, or trailers, suffer greatly in these storms. These lightweight homes are likely victims. The fast, swirling winds easily lift them up, twirl them around, and smash them down to the ground.

Television reports and newspaper accounts often show pictures of trailer homes wrecked by tornadoes. The pictures may make you think there is an attraction between these homes and tornadoes. But the storms just go wherever their twisting winds take them.

What was the most amazing escape from a tornado?

The escape of 12 children in China. On May 29, 1986, the children were on their way to school. As they walked along, a tornado sucked them up and carried them 12 miles (19 km) through the air. But then it gently dropped them down onto some nice, soft sand dunes. No one was hurt! You can imagine what their teacher thought when she heard this story!

This is an exaggerated diagram of the path of a tornado.

How do volcanoes affect the weather?

Some volcanoes hurl up huge amounts of dust. Winds carry the dust around the world. The dust can block sunlight and lower temperature. It can also help raindrops to form, causing more rainfall. Sometimes it takes months or years for all the dust from a major volcano to settle on the ground.

How can a large meteor affect the weather?

A big meteor smashing into Earth can send gigantic amounts of dust into the air. The results can be the same as an erupting volcano.

Many people believe that a giant meteor crashed into Earth about 65 million years ago. The impact changed the climate so much that it led to the extinction of the dinosaurs!

Can pollution affect the weather?

Yes. Dust from cars and factories causes added raindrops to form. You get more rain.

Sometimes gases and chemicals from factories join with water vapor in the air. They form acids that fall as acid rain. Acid rain can make trees die, lakes and rivers smell, and buildings crumble.

What is El Niño?

A warm current in the Pacific Ocean. El Niño (el-NEEN-yoh) flows southward along the west coast of South America around Christmas every year. But every five years or so it lasts longer than usual. Then the cold waters get very warm. This heats the air above them. And this means weather trouble for the whole world!

El Niño can lead to droughts in Australia and Africa. It can cause floods in North America, storms in California, and heavy rains in Ecuador and Peru.

How do meteorologists know what the weather will be?

They gather information on weather conditions from stations around the globe and satellites in space. Then they enter the data into supercomputers and draw special weather maps. Finally, they use all this information—and their understanding of changing weather patterns—to make their forecasts.

Meteorologists are very good at predicting the weather. Their one-day forecasts are correct more than three out of every four times!

Can groundhogs predict the weather?

Some people think so. They say that groundhogs wake from their winter sleep on February 2nd and come out of their holes in the ground. If it is sunny and the groundhog sees its shadow, it crawls back into its hole—and there will be six more weeks of winter. If it is cloudy and the groundhog sees no shadow, it stays out of its hole—and spring weather will soon come.

It's a fun idea. But meteorologists can find no connection between what the groundhog does and the coming of spring weather.

How can you tell tomorrow's weather today?

A few ways. Listen to reports on radio or television. Check weather maps for winds, air pressure, humidity, and storms in the area. Keep track of weather conditions on your own weather instruments. Become a good observer of clouds, winds, and other weather conditions.

In other words, wise up to the weather. That way, you'll never pick the wrong day for a picnic or get caught in the rain without an umbrella!

Index

About the Authors

The Bergers work at home. They start each day by listening to the weather report. They say, "Rainy days are great for writing. But snowstorms and hurricanes are definitely bad news. They play havoc with our computers and lights."

About the Illustrator

Robert Sullivan went to school for drawing and painting at The School of Visual Arts in New York City. But he has been creating artwork since before he was in kindergarten. Robert has also taken courses in meteorology and likes to watch the weather. He enjoyed painting the pictures in this book because he loves outdoor activities, especially cycling. Robert lives in Maine with his wife and daughter.